Remembrance Day

"Lest we forget"

Jill Foran

Weigl

Published by Weigl Educational Publishers Limited
6325 10 Street S.E.
Calgary, Alberta, Canada
T2H 2Z9

www.weigl.com
Copyright ©2010 Weigl Educational Publishers Limited

Library and Archives Canada Cataloguing in Publication data available upon request.
Fax 403-233-7769 for the attention of the Publishing Records department.

ISBN 978-1-55388-518-4 (hard cover)
ISBN 978-1-55388-523-8 (soft cover)

Printed in the United States of America
1 2 3 4 5 6 7 8 9 0 13 12 11 10 09

Editor: Heather C. Hudak
Design: Terry Paulhus

Weigl acknowledges Getty Images as one of its primary image suppliers for this title.
Newscom: page 9.

Contents

What is Remembrance Day? 4

Countries at War 6

The Role of Soldiers 8

Time to Remember 10

A Song of Remembrance 12

A Special Poem 14

A Symbol of Remembrance 16

War Memorials 18

Tomb of the Unknown Soldier 20

Flying Flags 22

Glossary/Index 24

What is Remembrance Day?

Remembrance Day takes place on November 11 each year. On this day, Canadians honour the men and women who have served in times of war, conflict, and peace around the world. It is also a time for Canadians to pay tribute to war veterans and think about the importance of peace and freedom in their lives.

Countries at War

Canadians have served in three major wars and many conflicts. World War I began in Europe in 1914 and ended in 1918. This was the first time in history that almost every country in the world took part in the same war. World War II began in 1939 and ended in 1945. Five years later, the Korean War began. This war came to an end in 1953.

The Role of Soldiers

Soldiers are men and women who serve in wars and conflicts. More than 116,000 Canadians died while serving in World War I, World War II, and the Korean War. Canadian soldiers also help keep peace. Thousands of Canadians have served in peacekeeping missions all over the world. More than 100 have died while trying to maintain peace.

9

Time to Remember

World War I fighting stopped in the eleventh hour of the eleventh day of the eleventh month in 1918. A year later, King George V of England made a request. He asked all of his subjects to stop their daily tasks at 11:00 am on November 11 and observe two minutes of silence. This silence was to honour those who served in the war. This tradition still takes place today.

10

A Song of Remembrance

Last Post is a song that is played on a bugle or trumpet. It is a farewell to soldiers who died. *Last Post* is played before the two minutes of silence at Remembrance Day services. Then, a song called *Reveille* is played. It tells how the memory of the dead lives on.

13

A Special Poem

Canadian Colonel John McCrae cared for soldiers in France and Belgium during World War I. He saw poppies growing around soldiers' graves in a city called Flanders and wrote the poem *In Flanders Fields*. Today, this poem is said at Remembrance Day services across Canada. It honours those who fought in World War I.

In Flanders Fields

In Flanders fields the poppies blow
Between the crosses, row on row,
That mark our place; and in the sky
The larks, still bravely singing, fly
Scarce heard amid the guns below.

We are the Dead. Short days ago
We lived, felt dawn, saw sunset glow,
Loved, and were loved, and now we lie
In Flanders fields.

Take up your quarrel with the foe:
To you from falling hands we throw
The torch; be yours to hold it high.
If ye break faith with us who die
We shall not sleep, though poppies grow
In Flanders fields.

A Symbol of Remembrance

Wearing handmade poppies reminds Canadians of the soldiers who were killed and buried in Flanders. In Canada, people began wearing poppies as a symbol of remembrance in 1921.

17

War Memorials

Many cities and towns have **monuments** for those who died at war. These monuments are called war memorials or cenotaphs. On Remembrance Day, people gather at memorials to honour Canadians who have fought for their country. The National War Memorial on Parliament Hill in Ottawa is a symbol of Canadians who fought in World War I and other wars.

18

Tomb of the Unknown Soldier

The **Tomb** of the Unknown Soldier is in front of the National War Memorial. The remains of a Canadian soldier who died in World War I are inside. His name is not known. The tomb honours other soldiers who have died for their country. It is a symbol of the peace and freedom Canada works to maintain.

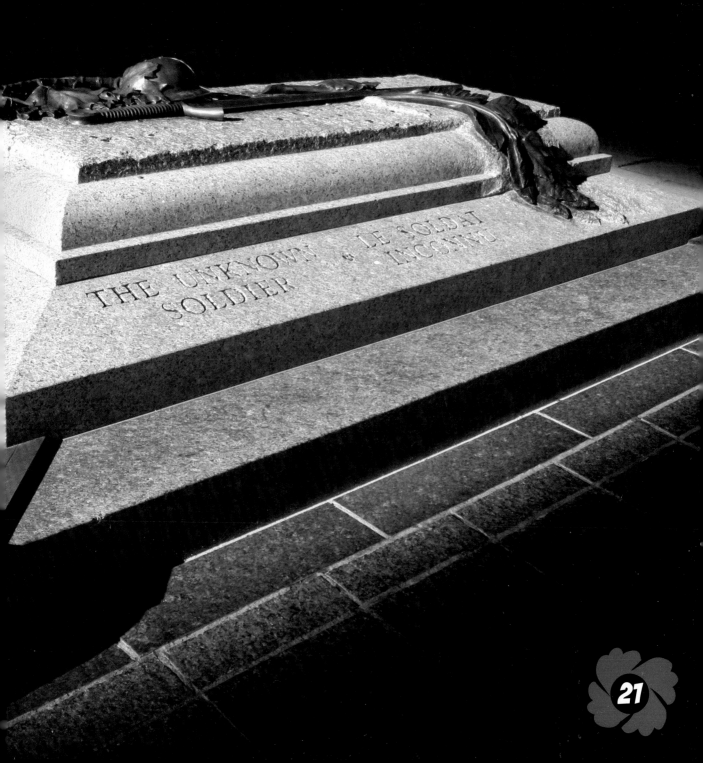

THE UNKNOWN SOLDIER · LE SOLDAT INCONNU

21

Flying Flags

Events take place across Canada on Remembrance Day. Flags do not fly at the top of their post, or mast. They fly at **half mast** to honour those who died in war. This means that flags are raised only halfway up their post.

23

Glossary

half mast	monuments
![flag at half mast]	![monument]
soldiers	**tomb**
![soldier]	![tomb]

Index

Last Post 12

National War
  Memorial 18, 20

poppies 14, 15, 16

soldiers 8, 12, 14,
  16, 20

Tomb of the
  Unknown Soldier 20